MISSISSIPPI

in words and pictures

BY DENNIS B. FRADIN

ILLUSTRATIONS BY RICHARD WAHL

MAPS BY LEN W. MEENTS

Consultant:
Caroline Killens, Librarian
Mississippi Department of
Archives and History

 CHILDRENS PRESS, CHICAGO

For my friend, Priscilla Stadig,
a Northern belle

For their help, the author thanks:
Jay K. Johnson, Assistant Professor of Anthropology, University of Mississippi
Ann Thompson, Choctaw Agency
Bonnie K. Martin, Program Assistant, Branch of Education, Choctaw Agency
Mississippi Museum of Natural Science
Charles Brown, Controller, Delta and Pine Land Company

Cypress Swamp

Picture Acknowledgments:
STATE OF MISSISSIPPI—cover, pages 2, 7, 9, 11, 13, 18, 19, 20, 21, 22,
25, 26, 27, 29, 30, 32, 33, 34, 35, 36, 37, 39, 40, 41, 43
JAMES P. ROWAN—pages 14(2), 23
DEPARTMENT OF THE ARMY, CORPS OF ENGINEERS, MOBILE
DISTRICT—page 16
NASA—page 42
COVER—D'Evereux

1 2 3 4 5 6 7 8 9 10 11 12 R 87 86 85 84 83 82 81 80

Library of Congress Cataloging in Publication Data

Fradin, Dennis B
    Mississippi in words and pictures.

    SUMMARY: Presents an introduction to the history,
geography, industry, places of interest, and people of
the "Magnolia State."
    1. Mississippi—Juvenile literature.   [1. Mississi-
ppi]   I. Wahl, Richard, 1939-   II. Meents, Len W.
III. Title.
F341.3.F72   976.2   80-36855
ISBN 0-516-03924-5

Mississippi (miss • iss • IP • ee) was named for the Mississippi River. The state lies deep in the South. Mississippi was once a big cotton-growing state. Cotton is still grown there. But soybeans and many other crops are grown now.

In Mississippi today more people work in factories than on farms. Ships and airplanes are made in the state. Foods are packaged. Clothes are made. Trees are cut down in Mississippi's forests and then made into wood products.

Do you know where Jefferson Davis, the president of the Confederacy, lived as a cotton planter? Or where the Battle of Vicksburg was fought? Do you know where the writer William Faulkner was born? Or the singer Elvis Presley? If you haven't guessed, the answer to these questions is: Mississippi!

Millions of years ago, the land was covered by water.
Sharks swam about. So did whales. Their teeth and bones
have been found in places that are now dry land.

The first people came to Mississippi at least 11,000
years ago. At first people hunted. Later they learned to
farm.

One early Indian group is called the *Mound Builders*.

They first lived here about 3,000 years ago. They built many dirt hills, or mounds, in Mississippi. Some of the mounds were used to bury the dead. Houses and temples were built on top of other mounds. Sometimes the Mississippi River flooded. High mounds were built near the river. During floods, people may have kept from drowning by standing on these mounds.

In more recent times, many Indian tribes lived in Mississippi. The Chickasaw (CHICK • ah • saw), Choctaw (CHOCK • taw), and Natchez (NAT • chez) were three of the main tribes. In all, there were about 30,000 Indians in Mississippi.

In Mississippi's rich soil the Indians grew corn, beans, and pumpkins. The Indians speared fish in Mississippi's many rivers. Mississippi has huge forests of pines and other trees. The Indians cut down trees and built log houses. They hunted deer, bears, and bison in the forests. The meat was eaten. The skins were used to make clothes.

The Indians of Mississippi enjoyed sports. They played a game much like lacrosse. The ball was made of deerskin. The racquets and goals were wood. The Indians also enjoyed music and storytelling. According to a Natchez story, the sun made the first man. The Natchez worshipped the sun. They called their chief the "Great Sun."

Hernando de Soto (her • NAN • doh dih SO • toh) of Spain was the first explorer known to enter Mississippi. He arrived in 1540 while on a long search for gold. In his search, De Soto discovered the Mississippi River. He died of a fever in 1542 and was buried in the Mississippi River.

De Soto had planted the Spanish flag in Mississippi. But since gold was not found there, Spain had little interest in settling Mississippi.

Dressed in French and Indian costumes, modern-day Mississippians reenact the landing of the French at Ocean Springs.

The French were the first non-Indians to settle there. In 1682 the French explorer La Salle (la SAL) came by canoe down the Mississippi River. He claimed a huge area, including Mississippi, for France. The French formed their first colony in Mississippi in 1699. It was built at Old Biloxi (bill • OX • ee) — which is now called Ocean Springs. In 1716 the French built a settlement that became Natchez.

From 1754 to 1763 the French, the Indians, and the English fought a war in America. It was called the French and Indian War. The English won. Now England ruled Mississippi and other lands in America. But not for very long!

A new country was formed in America in 1776. It was called the United States of America. By 1798 much of Mississippi belonged to the United States. It wasn't a state yet. It was a *territory*—land owned by the United States.

Mississippi has some of the richest soil in the world. By the thousands, Americans came to Mississippi to farm. Many came by wagon. Others came by flatboat down the Mississippi River. People, cows, and chickens traveled together on the flatboats. Once in Mississippi, the people built wooden houses. They set up farms. Many planted cotton.

Above: Close-up of a cotton plant
Left: Today, machines are used to pick cotton.

Cotton grows well where it is warm. It needs rich soil. It needs good rainfall. Mississippi was perfect. By 1800 cotton was the main crop in Mississippi.

At this time, many clothes were made of cotton. Cotton was so important that it was called "King Cotton." Mississippi was important because so much cotton was grown there.

Some cotton growers became very rich. They built huge farms, called *plantations* (plan • TAY • shunz). Black slaves did the work on the plantations.

Meanwhile, the Indians grew angry as Americans took their lands. Some Indians fought. But there were too many soldiers and settlers against them. The Indians were forced to sign treaties. Most were moved out of Mississippi.

As fighting with the Indians ended, more settlers moved to Mississippi. Many wanted Mississippi to become a state. On December 10, 1817, Mississippi became our 20th state. In 1822 Jackson became the capital of Mississippi. The state was nicknamed the *Magnolia* (mag • NOHL • yuh) *State* because of its lovely magnolia trees.

The early 1800s were good times for cotton planters. They made lovely gardens around their plantation houses. They raced horses. They held dances. "Do you remember how we came to Mississippi on flatboats?"

The *Delta Queen*, an antique paddle wheel steamboat, still carries passengers up and down the Mississippi River.

they reminded each other. By the 1830s steamboats carried people—and cotton—on the river. Some steamboats were so fancy that they were like floating palaces. Cotton planters went to New Orleans, Louisiana (loo • EE • zee • AN • ah). There they sold their cotton. The cotton was then sent to northern cities or England where it was made into clothes.

More and more slaves were brought in to work on the cotton plantations. By 1840 there were more slaves than white people in Mississippi.

Americans began to argue about slavery. People in Mississippi and the other Southern states feared that the United States government would end slavery. Southerners didn't want that to happen.

Southerners had other complaints. They bought goods from Europe. The United States government made them pay high taxes on these goods. Southerners spoke of "States' Rights." They wanted each state to decide for itself about slavery and taxes.

People in the North and South talked for years. The words solved nothing. Mississippi and the other Southern states broke away from the United States. In February of 1861 Southerners formed their own country. It was called the Confederate (kon • FED • uh • rit) States of America. Jefferson Davis, who had been a Mississippi senator, became the president of the Confederacy.

UNION STATES & TERRITORIES
BORDER STATES IN THE UNION
CONFEDERATE STATES

Statue of a Confederate soldier

Fighting between the Confederate (Southern) and
Union (Northern) states began in April of 1861. This was
the start of the Civil War.

Mississippi sent about 80,000 men to fight for the
South. There were a number of Civil War battles in
Mississippi. The biggest was the Battle of Vicksburg.
Vicksburg is on the Mississippi River. The North
controlled most of the river. It wanted to control all of it.
Northern soldiers surrounded Vicksburg. They shelled
the city for 47 days in 1863.

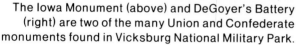

The Iowa Monument (above) and DeGoyer's Battery (right) are two of the many Union and Confederate monuments found in Vicksburg National Military Park.

The people of Vicksburg couldn't get food. Some had to eat mules and cats to survive. Some hid in caves to escape the bullets. Finally, the Northern soldiers took the city. The North had won a big Civil War battle. It was now in control of the Mississippi River. It could send shipments on the Mississippi River and stop Southern shipments on the river.

The North had more supplies. It had more soldiers and more weapons. By 1865 the North won the Civil War.

Like much of the South, Mississippi was in ruins. About 60,000 young men from Mississippi had been killed or wounded in the war. Plantations were smashed. Railroads were wrecked. The capital city, Jackson, had been burned. Since Jackson had little more than chimneys left standing, people called it "Chimneyville" (CHIM • nee • vill). Other Mississippi cities were burned. To make things worse, the people did not have their own government. Northern lawmakers ruled Mississippi for about ten years.

In 1870, Mississippi again became part of the United States. Mississippians (miss • iss • IP • eey • ans) slowly rebuilt their state. They didn't just rebuild cities. They had to form a new way of life. With the slaves freed, the plantation system ended. Cotton was no longer "King." People still farmed. Many were *sharecroppers*. They rented land, and had to share their crops with the landowners. Most sharecroppers were poor. But they did begin growing many kinds of crops.

Oysters, caught in the Gulf of Mexico, are brought to Biloxi Harbor.

Mississippians turned to other work besides farming. They looked to their forests. They saw that the state had "green gold" in its pines and other trees. Trees were cut down. In factories, the lumber was made into furniture and other wood products.

The Gulf of Mexico touches the southeast edge of Mississippi. Shrimp and oysters were taken from the gulf. Fishing grew as a business.

Workers in a shipbuilding yard in Ingalls

Throughout the 1900s, many factories were built in Mississippi. In these factories, farmers' crops and seafood are packaged as food. Cotton is made into clothes. Ships are built. Today, more Mississippi people work in factories than on farms. Manufacturing (making things) has become bigger than farming in the state.

There were growing problems between people in the 1900s. Often, black and white people were separated by a wall of hatred. Blacks were kept out of some jobs. They had to go to separate schools. They were kept out of some neighborhoods. They were stopped from voting.

Some Mississippians—black and white—worked to change things. Sometimes, the hatred was so great that people were killed. A black leader named Medgar Evers (MED • gur EV • ers) worked to get black Mississippians to vote. In 1963 he was shot to death. In 1964 three young men were working for the rights of black people. They were killed near Philadelphia (fill • ah • DEL • fee • yah), Mississippi.

Things did change. By the 1960s many Mississippi schools had black and white children. Blacks were elected as lawmakers. In 1969 Charles Evers (the brother of Medgar) was elected mayor of Fayette.

Today, Mississippi lawmakers are working to improve life for all the state's people. They are working to make better schools. They are working to bring more businesses to the Magnolia State. They are working to make sure Mississippi's air, water, and land will always be beautiful.

You have learned about some of Mississippi's history. Now it is time for a trip—in words and pictures— through the Magnolia State.

Pretend you are in an airplane high above Mississippi. Do you see that big river on Mississippi's western border? That is the Mississippi River. Across the river to the west are the states of Arkansas and Louisiana. Louisiana and the body of water known as the Gulf of Mexico are to the south. Alabama is to the east. Tennessee is north of Mississippi.

Barge traffic on the Mississippi River

Skyline of Jackson and the new state capitol

Your airplane is landing in a big city. You have arrived in Jackson. It has the most people of any Mississippi city. It is also the capital of the state.

Once, Choctaw Indians lived here. Jackson was picked to be state capital in 1821. It was named after a United States president, Andrew Jackson.

Visit the old capitol, in Jackson. This was where Mississippi lawmakers met in the 1800s. Today, the State Historical Museum is inside. There you can learn about the history of the state.

Visit the new capitol. This is where Mississippi lawmakers have met since 1903.

Above: City Hall
Top left: Railroad yard
Left: The old capitol is now the State
    Historical Museum.

Machinery, clothes, and furniture are made in Jackson.
These products go by train and truck to other cities in
America. So many highways and trains go through
Jackson that it is nicknamed the *Crossroads of the
South.*

Above: The Chimneyville Choo-Choo in
Jackson's Zoological Park.
Right: State Coliseum

Do you remember how people once called this city
"Chimneyville"? If only they could see the big new
buildings in Jackson today! The State Coliseum (col • ih •
SEE • um) is a huge, round building. Sports and musical
concerts are held there.

Would you like to see fossils and learn about plants
and animals? You can, at the Mississippi Museum of
Natural Science in Jackson. Jackson has art museums
and a fine orchestra. It also has a zoo where you can see
monkeys, lions, and many other animals. The zoo has a
special children's area where you can pet goats and
sheep.

Jackson is home to many fine schools. Jackson State University is there. So is the University of Mississippi Medical Center. There people study to be doctors, dentists, and nurses.

Near Jackson you can see some very strange trees. Long ago, water carried the trees here from the far north. Minerals in the water turned the trees to stone. The stone trees are called the *petrified forest.*

About 45 miles west of Jackson visit Vicksburg. You can still see buildings hit by cannonballs during the Battle of Vicksburg. About 20,000 people were killed or wounded in this battle.

Graves in Vicksburg National Military Park

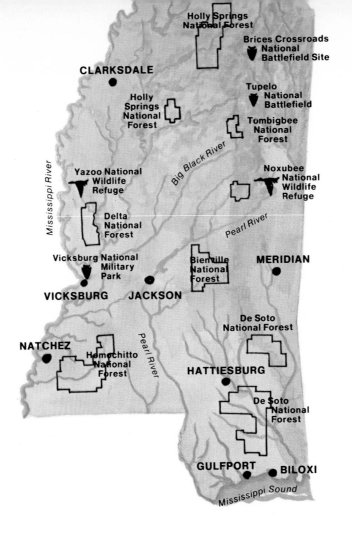

From Vicksburg, you might take a boat ride on the Mississippi River. The Mississippi River is very wide. It is also the longest river in the United States. The word *Mississippi* is an Indian word meaning "Father of Waters." When people want to see if you can spell, they may ask you to spell Mississippi. If people ask you, tell them. Then ask them if *they* know what the word means!

The land along the Mississippi River is called the *Delta* (DEL • tah). It has great soil. The soil was brought there by the river in times of floods. You will see many cotton fields along the Delta. Mississippi is still a leading cotton-growing state. Now you'll also see corn, rice, and soybeans growing on the Delta.

About 70 miles south of Vicksburg you will come to Natchez. Natchez is the oldest city on the Mississippi River. It was founded as a fort by the French in 1716.

Left: Natchez Bridge
Right: A fork lift loads bales of cotton

Stanton Hall

Long ago, wealthy people in the cotton business lived in and near Natchez. You can still see many of their houses. Stanton Hall and D'Evereux (dev • ER • oh) are two big houses you can visit.

Long ago, a trail led from Natchez all the way to Nashville, Tennessee. People traveled by horseback on the trail. It was called the Natchez Trace. Today, a parkway has been built over this famous old trail.

Oil refinery at sunset

Near Natchez you'll see many oil wells. Oil was discovered in Mississippi in 1939. Since then, southern Mississippi has become a big oil-producing area. Oil is used to run cars and machinery. Natural gas is also found in southern Mississippi. It is used to heat houses and cook food. Mississippi is a leading state for producing both oil and natural gas.

Head down into southeast Mississippi. This part of the state lies along the waters of the Gulf of Mexico. The land along the water is known as the *Gulf Coast*.

Many people come to the Gulf Coast to vacation. It has sandy beaches. It has warm weather. In January, it can be 70° on the beaches. But when the weather is bad on the Gulf Coast it can be terrible. Huge storms known as *hurricanes* have hit this area. One hurricane in 1957 killed 390 people in Mississippi, Texas, and Louisiana. Another in 1969 had winds up to 170 miles per hour. Today, satellites in space take pictures of hurricanes. People are warned when one is coming.

As you travel along the Gulf Coast you'll see fishing boats. Mississippi is a leading state for catching shrimp. Oysters, crabs, and red snappers are other seafoods caught in the gulf.

Visit Biloxi, on the Gulf Coast in southeast Mississippi. Biloxi was founded in 1717. The name *Biloxi* is an Indian word meaning "first people." Today, this old city is a big vacation area. It is also one of Mississippi's larger cities.

Above: Biloxi Lighthouse
Top left: Fishing boats
Left: Close-up of shrimp

The Biloxi Lighthouse is a lovely sight. It has helped guide boats to shore since 1848. Boats in the Biloxi area bring back shrimp and oysters These are packaged as food in Biloxi.

Fort Massachusetts

Gulfport is right next to Biloxi. It, too, is a big vacation city. People enjoy sailing and deep-sea fishing in the Gulfport-Biloxi area. You might enjoy a boat ride from either city. You can go out to Ship Island. You'll see Fort Massachusetts (mass • ah • CHOO • setts) there. The Union army used this as a prison during the Civil War.

Long ago, pirates sailed near Ship Island and other Mississippi islands. Pirates were known to hide in the swamps of southern Mississippi. There are even stories of pirate treasures buried in Mississippi.

Pirate ships aren't built in Mississippi. But many other ships are. Pascagoula (pass • kah • GOO • lah), which is near Mississippi's southeast corner, is a big shipbuilding city.

The Pascagoula River flows into Pascagoula. This river is nicknamed the "Singing River." In places, it makes a noise that sounds like singing. No one knows why. The Indians had a story to explain it. They said that, long ago, the Pascagoula Indians were about to be attacked by the Biloxi Indians. The Pascagoula were a gentle people. They were outnumbered. Rather than die in battle, the Pascagoula Indians walked into the river. While singing their death songs, they drowned. Ever since, the Pascagoula River has made the singing sound.

Much of southern Mississippi is covered by pine trees. The pine forests are known as the "Piney Woods." Lots of lumber comes from this area. It provides wood for such products as houses.

Deer in the Piney Woods

If you hike through the Piney Woods and other Mississippi forests you'll see many animals. You'll see deer. You may see foxes. Beavers build their dams on streams and rivers in wooded areas. Alligators live in some swampy places. Quail and wild turkeys can also be seen.

Hattiesburg (HAT • eez • berg) is in the Piney Woods of southeast Mississippi. Hattiesburg was once a lumber mill city. Today, chemicals, clothes, and foods are made in Hattiesburg. You'll see a lot of college students in Hattiesburg. The University of Southern Mississippi and William Carey College are both there.

Above: The University of Southern Mississippi at Hattiesburg

Left: Jimmie Rodgers Memorial

Northeast of Hattiesburg you will come to Meridian (mer • ID • ee • yan). Meridian was formed in 1860, as railroads entered the area. For one month in 1863 Meridian was the capital of Mississippi. Today furniture and other wood products are made in Meridian.

Have you ever heard country music? Jimmie Rodgers, called the "Father of Country Music," was born in Meridian. "Train Whistle Blues" and "Mississippi Delta Blues" are just two of the songs he sang. At the Jimmie Rodgers Memorial and Museum you can learn about him.

At the Choctaw Indian Fair the Indians play the ball game of their ancestors.

Northwest of Meridian visit the Choctaw Indian reservation, near Philadelphia. About 4,000 Indians live in Mississippi today. The Choctaw are now the main tribe.

Some Choctaw work as teachers or storekeepers. Others build houses or work at many other jobs. But the Indians have not forgotten their traditions. Choctaw children are taught English as well as the Indian language. Parents and grandparents teach children the stories of their people. Children learn to make baskets and do beadwork.

Once a year, the Choctaw Indian Fair is held in Philadelphia. The Indians perform the Rabbit Dance and the Snake Dance. They play the ball games that their people played so long ago.

After seeing the Indian reservation, head up into northern Mississippi. You'll see a lot of farms. Many crops—such as corn, cotton, and oats—are grown here. Many kinds of livestock are raised in this area. You'll see beef cattle. You'll see cows that give milk. Hogs and chickens are also raised in northern Mississippi.

Cattle are an important part of Mississippi's economy.

Northern Mississippi has hills. It has lakes and ponds where people swim and fish. It has many small towns, with pretty names. Blue Mountain, Sunflower, Swan Lake, and Pontotoc are just four of them.

Northern Mississippi also is home to the University of Mississippi, which is near Oxford. People in Mississippi call this school "Ole Miss."

Visit the city of Greenville, on the Mississippi River. Wood products are made in Greenville. So are cotton products.

Right: This sign welcomes visitors to the "Ole Miss" campus.
Below: The library is the "heart" of the university.

Above: The Ross R. Barnett Reservoir is used for
fishing and other water sports
Left: Construction on the Tenn-Tom Waterway

Greenville was flooded by the Mississippi many times.
In 1927 much of the town was underwater. The people
didn't want to move the town. So they moved the river!
It was done by blocking the water so that it would flow
on a new course.

Floods of the Mississippi River have wiped some towns
off the map. There are towns where people once lived
that now lie under the river. Big dirt walls called *levees*
(LEV • eez) have been built in many places. They now
keep the river from flooding towns and farms.

To finish your Mississippi trip visit the Delta and Pine Land Company Plantation, not far from Greenville. Its cotton fields remind you of the old Mississippi, when cotton was "King." But today machines plant and pick the cotton. They remind you of the new Mississippi—a place of machines and factories as well as farms.

Places don't tell the whole story of Mississippi. Many interesting people have lived in the Magnolia State.

Greenwood Leflore (lih • FLOR) (1800-1865) was born near where Jackson now stands. He became a Choctaw Indian Chief. Chief Greenwood Leflore helped form schools for Indian children. Most of the Choctaw were forced to leave Mississippi. But Chief Greenwood Leflore worked to allow some to stay. The city of Greenwood, Mississippi, was named for him.

Jefferson Davis (1808-1889) was born in Kentucky. He moved to Mississippi as a child. He became a cotton

Beauvoir

planter. He also became a soldier and a Mississippi
lawmaker. When the Confederate States of America was
formed, Davis was elected president. He led the South
during the Civil War. Jefferson Davis spent his last 12
years in Mississippi. He lived in a house called Beauvoir
(bow • VWAR) in Biloxi. He wrote *The Rise and Fall of
the Confederate Government* there.

Nathan Bedford Forrest (1821-1877) was born in
Tennessee. He, too, became a Mississippi cotton planter.
During the Civil War, Forrest was a great Confederate
general. At the battle of Brice's Cross Roads, in
Mississippi, the Union had more men than Forrest.

William Faulkner won the Noble Prize in 1949.

Leading soldiers on horseback, Forrest attacked very quickly. Under him, the Confederates won this battle. General Forrest was wounded a number of times, but he lived through the Civil War.

Hiram R. Revels (HI • rem REV • elz) (1822-1901) was born in North Carolina. He became a minister. He formed schools for blacks. From 1870 to 1871 Revels was a United States senator from Mississippi. He was the first black to serve as a U.S. senator.

William Faulkner (FAWK • ner) (1897-1962) was born in New Albany, Mississippi. Faulkner became a writer. *Go Down, Moses* is just one of his books. He is remembered as one of the greatest American writers of all time.

Eudora Welty (you • DOR • ah WEL • tee) was born in Jackson, Mississippi, in 1909. She became a great writer, too. She wrote short stories about life in small towns in the South.

Did you ever hear of the playwright Tennessee Williams? He wasn't born in Tennessee. He was born in Columbus, Mississippi, in 1911. *Cat on a Hot Tin Roof* is just one of his plays.

Mississippi has also produced a number of musicians. Leontyne (LEE • on • tine) Price was born in Laurel, Mississippi, in 1927. As a girl, she sang in her church choir. Leontyne Price became an opera star.

Elvis Presley (1935-1977) was born in Tupelo (TOO • pel • oh), Mississippi. He sang in his church choir, too. He

Birthplace of Elvis Presley

taught himself to play the guitar. Elvis Presley once made a record as a surprise for his mother. People in the record business heard it and liked it. Elvis Presley became one of the most popular singers of all time.

Fred Wallace Haise, Jr. was born in Biloxi in 1933. He became an astronaut. In 1970 he and two other men were headed for the moon. There was an explosion in the spacecraft 206,000 miles from Earth! The astronauts had no electricity. They had no air. Haise and the two others got into the little ship that was supposed to land on the moon. In it, they returned safely to Earth.

Earth as seen from outer space

Longwood in Natchez

The land of Mound Builders . . . Indian tribes . . . cotton plantations . . . and Civil War battles.

Home to Jefferson Davis . . . William Faulkner . . . and Elvis Presley.

Once a great cotton-growing state.

Now a state that combines farming and manufacturing.

This is Mississippi—the Magnolia State.

Facts About MISSISSIPPI

Area—47,716 square miles (32nd biggest state)

Greatest Distance North to South—352 miles

Greatest Distance East to West—188 miles

Borders—Tennessee to the north; Alabama to the east; the Gulf of Mexico and
  Louisiana to the south; Louisiana and Arkansas to the west across the
  Mississippi River

Highest Point—806 feet above sea level (Woodall Mountain)

Lowest Point—Sea level along the coast of the Gulf of Mexico

Hottest Recorded Temperature—115° (at Holly Springs, on July 29, 1930)

Coldest Recorded Temperature—Minus 19° (at Corinth, on January 30, 1966)

Statehood—Our 20th state, on December 10, 1817

Origin of Name Mississippi—Named for the the Mississippi River; *Mississippi*
  is an Indian word meaning "Father of Waters"

Capital—Jackson (became capital in 1822)

Previous Capitals—Natchez (1798-1802), Washington (1802-1817), Natchez
  (1817-1821), and Columbia (1821-1822)

Counties—82

U.S. Senators—2

U.S. Representatives—5

State Senators—52

State Representatives—122

State Song—"Go Mississippi" by Houston Davis

State Motto—*Virtute et armis* (Latin meaning "By valor and arms")

Main Nickname—The Magnolia State

Other Nicknames—The Bayou State, the Dairyland of Dixie

State Seal—Adopted in 1817

State Flag—Adopted in 1894

Coat-of-Arms of Mississippi—designed in 1894

State Flower—Flower of the magnolia (selected by Mississippi schoolchildren
  in 1900)

State Tree—Magnolia

State Bird—Mockingbird

State Land Mammal—White-tailed deer

State Water Mammal—Bottlenosed dolphin

State Fish—Largemouth bass

State Shell—Oyster shell

State Waterfowl—Wood duck

Main River—Mississippi River

Some Other Rivers—Big Black, Homochitto, Pascagoula, Pearl, Tennessee,
  Tombigbee, Yazoo

Some Islands—Cat, Horn, Petit Bois, Round, Ship

State Parks—17

National Forests—6

Animals—Deer, beavers, foxes, opossums, rabbits, squirrels, raccoons,
   alligators, many kinds of snakes and turtles, quail, ducks, wild turkeys, gulls,
   pelicans, sparrows, mockingbirds, woodpeckers, many other kinds of birds

Fishing—Shrimp, oysters, menhaden, red snappers, catfish, buffalo fish, carp

Farm Products—Beef cattle, milk, soybeans, cotton, rice, sweet potatoes, corn,
   hay, hogs, sheep, broiler chickens, eggs, turkeys, tomatoes, potatoes,
   apples, peaches, watermelons, strawberries, pecans

Mining—Oil, natural gas, clays, sand, gravel

Manufacturing Products—Ships, airplanes, and other transportation
   equipment; many kinds of canned, frozen, and packaged foods; chemicals;
   clothes; lumber; furniture; other wood products; paper products;
   machinery; textiles; clay products; glass products

Population—2,389,000 (1977 estimate)

Major Cities—

Jackson	190,700	(all 1979 estimates)
Biloxi	44,700	
Gulfport	44,700	
Meridian	44,400	
Greenville	43,000	
Hattiesburg	39,900	
Pascagoula	31,700	
Vicksburg	31,400	

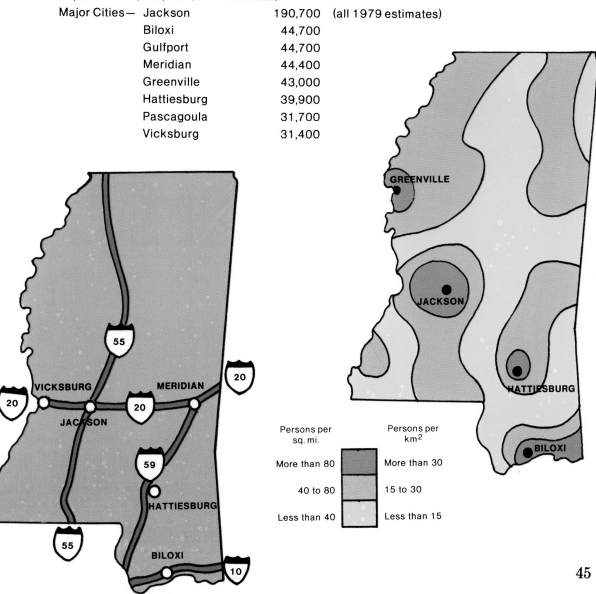

Persons per sq. mi.

More than 80

40 to 80

Less than 40

Persons per km²

More than 30

15 to 30

Less than 15

45

MISSISSIPPI HISTORY

There have been people in Mississippi for at least 11,000 years.

1540—Spanish explorer De Soto enters Mississippi

1699—Pierre le Moyne, Sieur d' Iberville, founds Old Biloxi (now Ocean Springs); this is the first French colony in Mississippi

1716—French build Fort Rosalie, which grows into the city of Natchez

1763—After French and Indian War, Mississippi now belongs to England

1798—Mississippi becomes a United States territory; Natchez is the capital of the Mississippi Territory

1817—Mississippi becomes our 20th state on December 10

1822—Jackson becomes the capital of Mississippi

1830—By the Treaty of Dancing Rabbit Creek, the Choctaw Indians give up their lands; some Choctaw stay in Mississippi, however

1844—University of Mississippi is founded

1858—Mississippi starts a program to improve farming by draining swamps in the Delta

1860—Population of the state is 791,305

1861—On January 9, Mississippi secedes from (leaves) the United States; the Civil War begins on April 12; Mississippi sends about 80,000 men to fight on the side of the South

1863—Northern forces take Vicksburg in the Battle of Vicksburg

1864—Although outnumbered, Southerners under General Nathan Bedford Forrest win the battle at Brice's Cross Roads

1865—Civil War ends; about 60,000 Mississippians were killed or wounded

1870—Mississippi is once again part of the United States

1889—Jefferson Davis, a Mississippi man who had been the Confederate president, dies on December 6

1890—Present state constitution is adopted

1900—Population of Magnolia State is 1,551,270

1903—New state capitol is completed at Jackson

1914-1918—During World War I, about 66,000 men and women from Mississippi are in U.S. uniforms

1917—Happy 100th birthday, Magnolia State!

1927—Terrible Mississippi River flood

1936—Laws are passed to help bring more manufacturing to the state

1939—Oil is found at Tinsley

1939-1945—During World War II, over 202,000 Mississippi men and women are in uniform

1949—William Faulkner, who had been born in New Albany, Mississippi, wins the Nobel Prize for Literature

1957—Hurricane Audrey hits Mississippi, Louisiana, and Texas, killing 390 people

1963—Black leader Medgar Evers is shot to death at Jackson
1964—Three young civil rights workers are killed near Philadelphia,
Mississippi
1965—For the first time, more people work at manufacturing than at farming in
Mississippi
1969—Charles Evers (Medgar's brother) becomes the first black to be elected
mayor of a Mississippi city in about a century; Hurricane Camille
causes great damage in Mississippi
1970—Population of Magnolia State is 2,216,912
1980—Floods hit Mississippi

INDEX

47

INDEX, Cont'd

About the Author:

Dennis Fradin attended Northwestern University on a creative writing scholarship and graduated in 1967. While still at Northwestern, he published his first stories in *Ingenue* magazine and also won a prize in *Seventeen's* short story competition. A prolific writer, Dennis Fradin has been regularly publishing stories in such diverse places as *The Saturday Evening Post, Scholastic, National Humane Review, Midwest,* and *The Teaching Paper.* He has also scripted several educational films. Since 1970 he has taught second grade reading in a Chicago school—a rewarding job, which, the author says, "provides a captive audience on whom I test my children's stories." Married and the father of three children, Dennis Fradin spends his free time with his family or playing a myriad of sports and games with his childhood chums.

About the Artists:

Len Meents studied painting and drawing at Southern Illinois University and after graduation in 1969 he moved to Chicago. Mr. Meents works full time as a painter and illustrator. He and his wife and child currently make their home in LaGrange, Illinois.

Richard Wahl, graduate of the Art Center College of Design in Los Angeles, has illustrated a number of magazine articles and booklets. He is a skilled artist and photographer who advocates realistic interpretations of his subjects. He lives with his wife and two sons in Libertyville, Illinois.